A GREEN SOUND

A GREEN SOUND

Nature Writing from the Living Tradition of Unitarian Universalism

EDITED BY WILLIAM LACH

Skinner House Books
Boston, Massachusetts

ISBN 1-55896-301-4
Printed in the USA

Note: The Unitarian Universalist Association is committed to using gender-inclusive language in all of its publications. In the interest of historical authenticity, however, all material in this anthology appears in its original form.

10 9 8 7 6 5 4 3 2 1
99 98 97 96 95 94 93 92

Book design by William Lach

A Green Sound : nature writing from the living tradition of Unitarian Universalism / edited by William Lach.

     p. cm.

     1. Nature—Literary collections. 2. Unitarian Universalists. 3. American literature. 4. English literature. I. Lach, William, 1968-
PS509.N3G74 1992
810.8'036—dc20   92-20332
                                                CIP

CONTENTS

PREFACE

In the May Sarton poem "Summer Music," the speaker describes the vibrant colors of nature as "a green sound." Sarton's words inspire the reader with the splendor of nature, just as nature has inspired her to write the poem. When the reader reads this poem—or any piece of nature writing—a bond is forged not only between the writer and reader, but also between nature and humankind.

Diplomats, abolitionists, and painters were among the contributors I considered in my search for Unitarian and Universalist nature writing—while letters, novels, and essays were scoured for source material. The selections that were chosen are rich in the diversity of the Unitarian Universalist tradition. Included here is Thomas Jefferson's impassioned reverie on the natural wonders of Virginia, a sensitive letter by Beatrix Potter to one of her young readers, a fable about racism by National Urban League director Whitney Young, and a discourse by Robert Fulghum on the act of shoveling snow.

From a broad range of historical and cultural origins, each of the contributors in *A Green Sound* approaches the natural world from a different perspective. Each contributor, however different, illustrates the fact that we are and always have been inextricably a part of the earth.

—W. L.

WILLIAM CULLEN BRYANT

Bryant (1794-1878) was baptized a Unitarian in 1858. As well as being an accomplished poet, he was editor of the New York Evening Post *for much of his life.*

Green River

When breezes are soft and skies are fair,
I steal an hour away from study and care,
And hie me away to the woodland scene,
Where wanders the stream with waters of green,
As if the bright fringe of herbs on its brink
Had given their stain to the waves they drink;
And they, whose meadows it murmurs through,
Have named the stream from its own fair hue.

Yet pure its waters—its shallows are bright
With colored pebbles and sparkles of light,
And clear the depths where its eddies play,
And dimples deepen and whirl away,
And the plane-tree's speckled arms o'ershoot
The swifter current that mines its root,
Through whose shifting leaves, as you walk the hill,
The quivering glimmer of sun and rill
With a sudden flash on the eye is thrown,
Like the ray that streams from the diamond-stone.
Oh, loveliest there the spring days come,
With blossoms, and birds, and wild-bees' hum;
The flowers of summer are fairest there,
And freshest the breath of the summer air;
And sweetest the golden autumn day
In silence and sunshine glides away.

Yet, fair as thou art, thou shunnest to glide,
Beautiful stream! by the village side;
But windest away from the haunts of men,
To quiet valley and shaded glen;
And forest, and meadow, and slope of hill,

Around thee, are lonely, lovely, and still,
Lonely—save when, by thy rippling tides,
From thicket to thicket the angler glides;
Or the simpler comes, with basket and book,
For herbs of power on thy banks to look;
Or haply, some idle dreamer, like me,
To wander, and muse, and gaze on thee,
Still—save the chirp of birds that feed
On the river cherry and seedy reed,
And thy own wild music gushing out
With mellow murmur of fairy shout,
From dawn to the blush of another day,
Like traveller singing along his way.

That fairy music I never hear,
Nor gaze on those waters so green and clear,
And mark them winding away from sight,
Darkened with shade or flashing with light,
While o'er them the vine to its thicket clings,
And the zephyr stoops to freshen his wings,
But I wish that fate had left me free
To wander these quiet haunts with thee,
Till the eating cares of earth should depart,
And the peace of the scene pass into my heart;
And I envy thy stream, as it glides along
Through its beautiful banks in a trance of song.

Though forced to drudge for the dregs of men,
And scrawl strange words with the barbarous pen,
And mingle among the jostling crowd,
Where the sons of strife are subtle and loud—
I often come to this quiet place,
To breathe the airs that ruffle thy face,
And gaze upon thee in silent dream,
For in thy lonely and lovely stream
An image of that calm life appears
That won my heart in greener years.

May Evening

The breath of Spring-time at this twilight hour
 Comes through the gathering glooms,
And bears the stolen sweets of many a flower
 Into my silent rooms.

Where hast thou wandered, gentle gale, to find
 The perfumes thou dost bring?
By brooks, that through the wakening meadows wind,
 Or brink of rushy spring?

Or woodside, where, in little companies,
 The early wild-flowers rise,
Or sheltered lawn, where mid encircling trees,
 May's warmest sunshine lies?

Now sleeps the humming-bird, that, in the sun,
 Wandered from bloom to bloom;
Now, too, the weary bee, his day's work done,
 Rests in his waxen room.

Now every hovering insect to his place
 Beneath the leaves hath flown;
And, through the long night hours, the flowery race
 Are left to thee alone.

O'er the pale blossoms of the sassafras
 And o'er the spice-bush spray,
Among the opening buds, thy breathings pass,
 And come embalmed away.

Yet there is sadness in thy soft caress,
 Wind of the blooming year!
The gentle presence, that was wont to bless
 Thy coming, is not here.

Go, then; and yet I bid thee not repair,
 Thy gathered sweets to shed,
Where pine and willow, in the evening air,
 Sigh o'er the buried dead.

Pass on to homes where cheerful voices sound,
     And cheerful looks are cast,
And where thou wakest, in thine airy round,
     No sorrow of the past.

Refresh the languid student pausing o'er
     The learned page apart,
And he shall turn to con his task once more
     With an encouraged heart.

Bear thou a promise, from the fragrant sward,
     To him who tills the land,
Of springing harvests that shall yet reward
     The labors of his hand.

And whisper, everywhere, that Earth renews
     Her beautiful array,
Amid the darkness and the gathering dews,
     For the return of day.

SARA MOORES CAMPBELL

Campbell is a Unitarian Universalist minister and author of the 1990 UUA meditation manual, Into the Wilderness.

The Growing Season

"I am not religious," says my neighbor, as he hoes the rows between his beans and corn.

"Oh yes, you are," I say to myself.

To plant a seed is an act of faith.
To collect compost is a response of gratitude to the creator.
To water, fertilize, and mulch the ground is an expression of religious responsibility.
To kneel down and pull weeds is a prayer.
To harvest is to participate in the fullness and grace of the spirit.
To protect and replenish creation is to love God.

"I am not religious," says my neighbor.

Yes, you are, I say.

WILLIAM ELLERY CHANNING

Channing (1780-1842), known as the "apostle of Unitarianism," was founder of the American Unitarian Association.

from Christian Worship

My first liberty was used in roaming over the neighboring fields and shores; and, amid this glorious nature, that love of liberty sprang up which has gained strength within me to this hour. I early received impressions of the great and the beautiful, which I believe have had no small influence in determining my modes of thought and habits of life.

In this town I pursued for a time my studies of theology. I had no professor or teacher to guide me; but I had two noble places of study. One was yonder beautiful edifice, now so frequented and so useful as a public library, then so deserted that I spent day after day, and sometimes week after week, amidst its dusty volumes, without interruption from a single visitor.

The other place was yonder beach, the roar of which has so often mingled with the worship of this place, my daily resort, dear to me in the sunshine, still more attractive in the storm. Seldom do I visit now without thinking of the work which there, in the sight of that beauty, in the sound of those waves, was carried on in my soul.

No spot on earth has helped to form me so much as that beach. There I lifted up my voice in praise amidst the tempest. There, softened by beauty, I poured out my thanksgiving and contrite confessions. There, in reverential sympathy with the mighty power around me, I became conscious of power within. There struggling thoughts and emotions broke forth, as if moved to utterance by nature's eloquence of the winds and waves. There began a happiness surpassing all worldly pleasures, all gifts of fortune—the happiness of communing with the works of God.

E.[DWARD] E.[STLIN] CUMMINGS

Cummings (1894-1962) was the son of a Unitarian minister who was never ordained and a mother whose Unitarian heritage extended back to its early roots. His poems are known for their unconventional typography and punctuation—as well as for their beauty.

'maggie and milly and molly and may'

maggie and milly and molly and may
went down to the beach(to play one day)

and maggie discovered a shell that sang
so sweetly she couldn't remember her troubles,and

milly befriended a stranded star
whose rays five languid fingers were;

and molly was chased by a horrible thing
which raced sideways while blowing bubbles:and

may came home with a smooth round stone
as small as a world and as large as alone.

For whatever we lose(like a you or a me)
it's always ourselves we find in the sea

'i thank You God for most this amazing'

i thank You God for most this amazing
day:for the leaping greenly spirits of trees
and a blue true dream of sky;and for everything
which is natural which is infinite which is yes

(i who have died am alive again today,
and this is the sun's birthday;this is the birth
day of life and of love and wings:and of the gay
great happening illimitably earth)

how should tasting touching hearing seeing
breathing any—lifted from the no

8

of all nothing—human merely being
doubt unimaginable You?

(now the ears of my ears awake and
now the eyes of my eyes are opened)

RALPH WALDO EMERSON

Emerson (1803-1882) was minister of the Second Church of Boston, Unitarian. His essays, lectures, and poems remain cornerstones of the Transcendentalist movement and of American literature itself.

from Nature

To speak truly, few adult persons can see nature. Most persons do not see the sun. At least they have a very superficial seeing. The sun illuminates only the eye of the man, but shines into the eye and the heart of the child. The lover of nature is he whose inward and outward senses are still truly adjusted to each other; who has retained the spirit of infancy even into the era of manhood. His intercourse with heaven and earth becomes part of his daily food. In the presence of nature, a wild delight runs through the man, in spite of real sorrows. Nature says—he is my creature, and maugre all his impertinent griefs, he shall be glad with me. Not the sun or the summer alone, but every hour and season yields its tribute of delight; for every hour and change corresponds to and authorizes a different state of the mind, from breathless noon to grimmest midnight. Nature is a setting that fits equally well a comic or a mourning piece. In good health, the air is a cordial of incredible virtue. Crossing a bare common, in snow-puddles, at twilight, under a clouded sky, without having in my thoughts any occurrence of special good fortune, I have enjoyed a perfect exhilaration. I am glad to the brink of fear. In the woods, too, a man casts off his years, as the snake his slough, and at what period soever of life, is always a child. In the woods, is perpetual youth. Within these plantations of God, a decorum and sanctity reign, a perennial festival is dressed, and the guest sees not how he should tire of them in a thousand years. In the woods, we return to reason and faith. There I feel that nothing can befall me in life— no disgrace, no calamity (leaving me my eyes), which nature cannot repair.

9

Standing on the bare ground—my head bathed by the blithe air, and uplifted into infinite space—all mean egotism vanishes. I become a transparent eyeball; I am nothing; I see all; the currents of the Universal Being circulate through me; I am part or particle of God. The name of the nearest friend sounds then foreign and accidental: to be brothers, to be acquaintances—master or servant, is then a trifle and a disturbance. I am the lover of uncontained and immortal beauty. In the wilderness, I find something more dear and connate than in streets or villages. In the tranquil landscape, and especially in the distant line of the horizon, man beholds somewhat as beautiful as his own nature.

The greatest delight which the fields and woods minister, is the suggestion of an occult relation between man and the vegetable. I am not alone and unacknowledged. They nod to me, and I to them. The waving of the boughs in the storm is new to me, and old. It takes me by surprise, and yet is not unknown. Its effect is like that of a higher thought or a better emotion coming over me, when I deemed I was thinking justly or doing right.

Yet it is certain that the power to produce this delight does not reside in nature, but in man, or in a harmony of both. It is necessary to use these pleasures with great temperance. For, nature is not always tricked in holiday attire, but the same scene which yesterday breathed perfume and glittered as for the frolic of the nymphs, is overspread with melancholy to-day. Nature always wears the colors of the spirit.

SOPHIA LYON FAHS

Fahs (1876-1978) was a minister and a pioneering religious educator. She served as Editor of UUA Curriculum Materials for Religious Education from 1937 to 1961. The following excerpt from a children's book (published by Skinner House Books) makes evident her belief in self-directed education.

from Jesus the Carpenter's Son

It was a red-letter day when Jesus was able to go off alone with his father to work on the small plot of land the family owned on the hillside back of the house. There they had a garden of vegetables and a field of grain and a small vineyard. It was a fresh, clear morning in late October. For some days the autumn rains had been falling, and the earth, which had been baked hard by the hot summer sun, was now soft enough to plough. Joseph wished to get his field planted.

When the plow had been well harnessed to the yoke between the oxen, Joseph took hold of the wooden handle saying, "I will do the plowing, Jesus, and you may guide the oxen back and forth over the field."

When they had finished preparing the field, Joseph handed Jesus a bag full of barley seeds, saying, "Today you may try your hand at sowing the seed."

Proudly Jesus tied the open bag to his girdle so that he could reach it. With easy, strong steps he walked barefoot down the plowed land, and back. All the while he sang a song, partly with words and partly without, as with wide sweeps of his arm out and back, out and back, he scattered the seeds through his fingers.

Never had Jesus known quite the joy that came to him then. The broken soil seemed to change into a place of wonder, and the brown specks he was scattering upon it became living gifts more precious than silver, direct from the hands of the Creator.

When the planting was finished, he and his father sat in the shade of the old olive tree, and ate a lunch of bread and honey. Before their eyes rose range upon range of hills, green shading into a soft blue like the sky. The hilltops seemed to reach the horizon. Below them spread rolling meadows newly washed with rain, while, above, fleecy grey clouds speckled the sky. It was a day for dreaming and stretching one's thoughts.

ROBERT FULGHUM

Fulghum is author of the best-selling All I Really Need to Know I Learned in Kindergarten, *a book of reflections that grew out of biweekly columns for a Unitarian Universalist church newsletter. He is minister emeritus of the Edmonds Unitarian Universalist Church in the state of Washington.*

from All I Really Need to Know I Learned in Kindergarten

Man next door and I look upon one another with suspicion. He's a raker and a shoveler, as I see it. A troubler of the natural ways of the earth. Left over from the breed that conquered the wilderness. He thinks of me in simpler terms: lazy.

See, every week during the fall he's out raking little leaves into little piles. And every time it snows, he's out tormenting the white stuff with his shovel. Once, out of either eagerness or outrage, he even managed to shovel a heavy frost. "Can't let old Mother Nature get ahead of you," says he.

So I tell him he hasn't the sense God gave a stump. In a kind of careful way. Leaves have been falling down for thousands and thousands of years, I tell him. And the earth did pretty well before rakes and people, I tell him. Old Mother Nature put the leaves where she wanted them and they made more earth. We need more earth, I tell him. We're running out of it, I tell him. And snow—snow is not my enemy, I tell him. Snow is God's way of telling people to slow down and rest and stay in bed for a day. And besides, snow always solves itself. Mixes with the leaves to form more earth, I tell him.

His yard *does* look neat, I must admit—*if* neatness is important. And he didn't fall down getting to his car last snowtime, and I in fact did. And he is a good neighbor, even if he is a raker and a shoveler. I'm open-minded about this thing.

Still, my yard has an Oriental carpet of red and yellow and green and brown. And his doesn't. And I spent the same time he spent shoveling snow collecting it in bottles to mix with orange juice July next, and I taped the sound of it falling and then used the tape to wrap Christmas presents *(snow has lots of uses)*.

I gave him a bottle of vintage winter snow for Christmas, wrapped in some of that tape. He gave me a rake. We're giving each other lessons in the proper use of these tools. I think he's got no religion, and I'm trying to convert him. He thinks I've got too much, and he's trying to get me to back off.

But in the end, in the end, in the final end of it all—I win. For he and I—and even you—will become what the leaves and snow become, and go where the leaves and snow go—whether we rake or shovel or not.

MARGARET FULLER

Fuller (1810-1850) established herself as a social reformer and one of the leading literary critics of her time. These passages are from Summer on the Lakes, *a collection of essays describing travels in the American wilderness.*

from Summer on the Lakes

Rock River, Illinois

The river flows sometimes through these parks and lawns, then betwixt high bluffs, whose grassy ridges are covered with fine trees, or broken with crumbling stone, that easily assumes the forms of buttress, arch, and clustered columns. Along the face of such crumbling rocks, swallows' nests are clustered, thick as cities, and eagles and deer do not disdain their summits. One morning, out in the boat along the base of these rocks, it was amusing, and affecting too, to see these swallows put their heads out to look at us. There was something very hospitable about it, as if man had never shown himself a tyrant near them. What a morning that was! Every sight is worth twice as much by the early morning light. We borrow something of the spirit of the hour to look upon them.

* * *

Niagara, New York

We have been here eight days, and I am quite willing to go away. So great a sight soon satisfies, making us content with itself, and with what is less than itself. Our desires, once realized, haunt us again less readily. Having "lived one day," we would depart, and become worthy to live another.

We have not been fortunate in weather, for there cannot be too much, or too warm sunlight for this scene, and the skies have been lowering, with cold, unkind winds. My nerves, too much braced up by such an atmosphere, do not well bear the continual stress of sight and sound. For here there is no escape from the weight of a perpetual creation; all other forms and motions come and go, the tide rises and recedes, the wind, at its mightiest, moves in gales and gusts, but here is really an incessant, an indefatigable motion. Awake or asleep, there is no escape, still this rushing round you and through you. It is in this way I have most felt the grandeur—somewhat eternal, if not infinite.

13

ELIZABETH GASKELL

Gaskell (1810-1865) was the daughter of staunch Unitarians and the wife of a prominent Unitarian minister in Manchester, England. In many of her novels, she depicted the day-to-day realities of manufacturing life. Consequently, her characters often seek spiritual redemption in nature.

from Ruth

The garden lay close under the house; a bright spot enough by day; for in that soil, whatever was planted grew and blossomed in spite of neglect. The white roses glimmered out in the dusk all the night through; the red were lost in shadow. Between the low boundary of the garden and the hills swept one or two green meadows; Ruth looked into the grey darkness till she traced each separate wave of outline. Then she heard a little restless bird chirp out its wakefulness from a nest in the ivy round the walls of the house. But the mother-bird spread her soft feathers, and hushed it into silence. Presently, however, many little birds began to scent the coming dawn, and rustled among the leaves, and chirruped loud and clear. Just above the horizon, too, the mist became a silvery grey cloud hanging on the edge of the world; presently it turned shimmering white; and then, in an instant, it flushed into rose, and the mountain-tops sprang into heaven, and bathed in the presence of the shadow of God. With a bound, the sun of a molten fiery red came above the horizon, and immediately thousands of little birds sang out for joy, and a soft chorus of mysterious, glad murmurs came forth from the earth; the low whispering wind left its hiding-place among the clefts and hollows of the hills, and wandered among the rustling herbs and trees, waking the flower-buds to the life of another day.

from The Doom of the Griffiths

It had been a glorious summer, with bright, hot, sunny weather; and now the year was fading away as seasonably into mellow days, with mornings of silver mists and clear frosty nights. The blooming look of the time of flowers was past and gone; but instead there were even richer tints abroad in the sun-coloured leaves, the lichens, the golden-blossomed furze: if it was the time of fading, there was a glory in the decay.

MARNI P. HARMONY

Harmony is a Unitarian Universalist minister. The following prayer is taken from the 1987 UUA meditation manual, Exaltation.

'I say that it touches us'

I say that it touches us that our blood is sea water and our tears are salt, that the seed of our bodies is scarcely different from the same cells in a seaweed, and that the stuff of our bones is like the coral.

I say that the tide rolls in on us, whether we like it or no, and the sands of time keep running their intended course.

I say we have to go down into the wave's trough to find ourselves, and then ride her swell until we can see beyond ourselves into our neighbor's eye.

I say that we shall never leave the harbor if we do not hoist the sail.

I say that we have got to walk the waves as well as solid ground.

I say that anyone who goes without consciousness of this will remain chained to a rusty anchor.

May the journey find us worthy. Amen.

FRANCES ELLEN WATKINS HARPER

Harper (1825-1911) was a member of the First Unitarian Church of Philadelphia. Born free in Baltimore, this African-American woman was an accomplished novelist, poet, social activist, and orator.

The Crocuses

They heard the South wind sighing
    A murmur of the rain;
And they knew that Earth was longing
    To see them all again.

While the snow-drops still were sleeping
    Beneath the silent sod;
They felt their new life pulsing
    Within the dark, cold clod.

Not a daffodil nor daisy
    Had dared to raise its head;
Not a fairhaired dandelion
    Peeped timid from its bed;

Though a tremor of the winter
    Did shivering through them run;
Yet they lifted up their foreheads
    To greet the vernal sun.

And the sunbeams gave them welcome,
    As did the morning air
And scattered o'er their simple robes
    Rich tints of beauty rare.

Soon a host of lovely flowers
    From vales and woodland burst;
But in all that fair procession
    The crocuses were first.

First to weave for Earth a chaplet
    To crown her dear old head
And to beautify the pathway
    Where winter still did tread.

And their loved and white haired mother
    Smiled sweetly 'neath the tough,
When she knew her faithful children
    Were loving her so much.

from **Moses**

Let haughty rulers learn that men
Of humblest birth and lowliest lot have
Rights as sacred and divine as theirs, and they

Who fence in leagues of earth by bonds and claims
And title deeds, forgetting land and water,
Air and light are God's own gifts and heritage
For man—who throw their selfish lives between
God's sunshine and the shivering poor—
Have never learned the wondrous depth, nor scaled
The glorious height of this great central truth,
Around which clusters all the holiest faiths
Of earth. The thunder died upon the air,
The lightning ceased its livid play, the smoke
And darkness died away in clouds, as soft
And fair as summer wreaths that lie around
The setting sun, and Sinai stood a bare
And ragged thing among the sacred scenes
Of earth.

* * *

He stood upon the highest peak of Nebo,
And saw the Jordan chafing through its gorges,
Its banks made bright by scarlet blooms
And purple blossoms. The placid lakes
And emerald meadows, the snowy crest
Of distant mountains, the ancient rocks
That dripped with honey, the hills all bathed
In light and beauty; the shady groves
And peaceful vistas, the vines opprest
With purple riches, the fig trees fruit-crowned
Green and golden, the pomegranates with crimson
Blushes, the olives with their darker clusters,
Rose before him like a vision, full of beauty
And delight. Gazed he on the lovely landscape
Till it faded from his view, and the wing
Of death's sweet angel hovered o'er the mountain's
Crest, and he heard his garments rustle through
The watches of the night.

BRET HARTE

Harte (1836-1902) was author of many short stories written primarily about the American West. A close friend of Thomas Starr King, Harte attended Unitarian churches in San Francisco and New York.

from The Idyl of Red Gulch

With such unconscious intervals the monotonous procession of blue skies, glittering sunshine, brief twilights, and starlit nights passed over Red Gulch. Miss Mary grew fond of walking in the sedate and proper woods. Perhaps she believed, with Mrs. Stidger, that the balsamic odors of the firs "did her chest good," for certainly her slight cough was less frequent and her step was firmer; perhaps she had learned the unending lesson which the patient pines are never weary of repeating to heedful or listless ears. And so, one day, she planned a picnic on Buckeye Hill, and took the children with her. Away from the dusty road, the straggling shanties, the yellow ditches, the clamor of restless engines, the cheap finery of shop-windows, the deeper glitter of paint and colored glass, and the thin veneering which barbarism takes upon itself in such localities—what infinite relief was theirs! The last heap of ragged rock and clay passed, the last unsightly chasm crossed—how the waiting woods opened their long files to receive them! How the children—perhaps because they had not yet grown quite away from the breast of the bounteous Mother—threw themselves face downward on her brown bosom with uncouth caresses, filling the air with their laughter; and how Miss Mary herself—felinely fastidious and intrenched as she was in the purity of spotless skirts, collar, and cuffs—forgot all, and ran like a quested quail at the head of her brood, until, romping, laughing, and panting, with a loosened braid of brown hair, a hat hanging by a knotted ribbon from her throat, she came suddenly and violently, in the heart of the forest, upon—the luckless Sandy!

The explanations, apologies, and not overwise conversation that ensued, need not be indicated here. It would seem, however, that Miss Mary had already established some acquaintance with this ex-drunkard. Enough that he was soon accepted as one of the party; that the children, with that quick intelligence which Providence gives the helpless, recognized a friend, and played with his blond beard, and long silken mustache, and took other liberties—as the helpless are apt to do. And when he had built a fire against a tree, and had shown them other mysteries of wood-craft, their admiration knew no bounds. At the close of two such foolish, idle, happy hours he found himself lying at the feet of the schoolmistress, gazing dreamily in her face, as she sat upon the sloping hillside, weaving wreaths of laurel and syringa, in very much the same attitude as he had lain when first they met. Nor was the similitude greatly forced. The weakness of an easy, sensuous nature, that had found a dreamy exaltation in liquor, it is to be feared was now finding an equal intoxication in love....

So they sat there, undisturbed—the woodpeckers chattering over-head, and the voices of the children coming pleasantly from the hollow below. What they said matters little. What they thought—which might have been interesting—did not transpire. The woodpeckers only learned how Miss Mary was an orphan; how she left her uncle's house, to come to California, for the sake of health and independence; how Sandy was an orphan, too; how he came to California for excitement; how he had lived a wild life, and how he was trying to reform; and other details which, from a woodpecker's view-point, undoubtedly must have seemed stupid, and a waste of time. But even in such trifles was the afternoon spent; and when the children were again gathered, and Sandy, with a delicacy the schoolmistress well understood, took leave of them quietly at the outskirts of the settlement, it had seemed the shortest day of her weary life.

KIM CRAWFORD HARVIE

Harvie is a Unitarian Universalist minister. This prayer is taken from the 1987 UUA meditation manual, Exaltation. *It was inspired by Albert Schweitzer, who once said, "We ask a heart of compassion/and gentle hands/ and kindly words."*

'Great spirit of life'

Great spirit of life
We pray today for our animal friends,
Grateful for their companionship and devotion.
By our kindness to them,
May we be worthy of their love.

We pray also for pets who are gone from us,
But who brightened our days
And who comforted us by night.

We pray for animals unknown to us
Who are suffering,
For many that are hunted or deserted or tortured.
We ask for them pity and mercy.
And for those who handle them
We ask a heart of compassion, gentle hands, and kind words.

Help us to be true friends to the animals
And love them and keep them and bless them
All the days of our lives. Amen.

WILLIAM HAZLITT

Hazlitt (1778-1830), an Englishman, disappointed his father by rejecting a career in the Unitarian ministry. Close acquaintance of the writers William Wordsworth, Samuel Taylor Coleridge, and Charles Lamb, Hazlitt is acknowledged as a pioneer of literary criticism.

from On the Love of the Country

In our love of Nature, there is all the force of individual attachment, combined with the most airy abstraction. It is this circumstance which gives refinement, expansion, and wild interest to feelings of this sort, when strongly excited, which every one must have experienced who is a true lover of Nature. The sight of the setting sun does not affect me so much from the beauty of the object itself, from the glory kindled through the glowing skies, the rich broken columns of light, or the dying streaks of day, as that it indistinctly recalls to me numberless thoughts and feelings which, through many a year and season, I have watched his bright descent in the warm summer evenings, or beheld him struggling to cast a "farewel sweet" through the thick clouds of winter. I love to see the trees first covered with leaves in the spring, the primroses peeping out from some sheltered bank, and the innocent lambs running races on the soft green turf; because, at that birth-time of Nature, I have always felt sweet hopes and happy wishes—which have not been fulfilled! The dry reeds rustling on the side of a stream—the woods swept by the loud blast—the dark massy foliage of autumn—the grey trunks and naked branches of the trees in winter—the sequestered copse and wide extended heath—the warm sunny showers, and December snows—have all charms for me; there is no object, however trifling or rude, that has not, in some mood or other, found the way to my heart; and I might say, in the words of the poet,

> "To me the meanest flower that blows can give
> Thoughts that do often lie too deep for tears."

Thus Nature is a kind of universal home, and every object it presents to us an old acquaintance with unaltered looks.

> "Nature did ne'er betray
> The heart that lov'd her, but through all the years
> Of this our life, it is her privilege
> To lead from joy to joy."

For there is that consent and mutual harmony among all her works, one undivided spirit pervading them throughout, that, if we have once knit ourselves in hearty fellowship to any of them, they will never afterwards appear as strangers to us, but, which ever way we turn, we shall find a secret power to have gone out before us, moulding them into such shapes as fancy loves, informing them with life and sympathy, bidding them put on their festive looks and gayest attire at our approach, and to pour all their sweets and choicest treasures at our feet. For him, then, who has well acquainted himself with Nature's works, she wears always one face, and speaks the same well-known language, striking on the heart, amidst unquiet thoughts and the tumult of the world, like the music of one's native tongue heard in some far-off country.

THOMAS JEFFERSON

Jefferson (1743-1826) was a noted naturalist, scholar, and architect, as well as the third President of the United States. Jefferson often wrote of his commitment to Unitarianism in his letters, and stated that he believed that Unitarianism would soon "be the religion of the majority from north to south." Jefferson's Notes on the State of Virginia, excerpted below, is a comprehensive record of natural history of much of the early United States. Jefferson's passion for natural beauty occasionally overshadows his clinical tone, as in the following passage.

from Notes on the State of Virginia

The passage of the Patowmac through the Blue Ridge is perhaps one of the most stupendous scenes in nature. You stand on a very high point of land. On your right comes up the Shenandoah, having ranged along the foot of the mountain an hundred miles to seek a vent. On your left approaches the Patowmac, in quest of a passage also. In the moment of their junction they rush together against the mountain, rend it asunder, and pass off to the sea. The first glance of this scene hurries our senses into the opinion, that this earth has been created in time, that the mountains were formed first, that the rivers began to flow afterwards, that in this place particularly they have been dammed up by the Blue Ridge of mountains, and have formed an ocean which filled the whole valley; that continuing to rise they have at length broken over at this spot, and have torn the mountain down from its summit to its base. The piles of rock on each hand, but particularly on the Shenandoah, the evident marks of their disrupture and avulsion from their beds by the most powerful agents of nature, corroborate the impression. But the distant finishing which nature has given to the picture is of a very different character. It is a true contrast to the fore-ground. It is placid and delightful, as that is wild and tremendous. For the mountain being cloven asunder she presents to your eye, through the cleft, a small catch of smooth blue horizon, at an infinite distance in the plain country, inviting you, as it were, from the riot and tumult roaring around, to pass through the breach and participate of the calm below. Here the eye ultimately composes itself; and that way too the road happens actually to lead. You cross the Patowmac above the junction, pass along its side through the base of the mountain for three miles, its terrible precipices hanging in fragments over you, and within about 20 miles reach Frederic town and the fine country round that. This scene is worth a voyage across the Atlantic. Yet here, as in the neighbourhood of the natural bridge, are people who have passed their lives within half a dozen miles, and have never been to survey these monuments of a war between rivers and mountains, which must have shaken the earth itself to its center.

THOMAS STARR KING

King (1824-1864) never attended theological school but enjoyed tremendous popularity as a minister in Boston and San Francisco. An avid explorer, he was among the first tourists to visit Yosemite and the Sierra Nevada and write about his travels there. Bret Harte, a close friend, once referred to King's "magic vision."

from The Laws of Disorder

The minutest organizations on the earth's surface are so related to the largest and wildest forces of nature as to show wonderful delicacy and subtlety of law. When we see common plants and shrubs growing so easily, we have no idea how the general order of the globe and sky is toned to their necessities. With regard to a common wild-flower, we may see that the force of gravitation which holds its fibres in the earth and strengthens its stalk is graduated so that, while it supports a constellation, it shall not prevent the juices from rising through the cells to carry life to the leaves. So the bulk and heat of the sun, the constitution of the air, the size of the sea, the swiftness of the earth's whirling and the diameter of its orbit, are determined with admirable relation to its need of heat and rain and wind, its alternations of light and gloom, and the changes of seasons from spring to winter. An alteration even of a slight percentage in the mixture and partnership of these great forces would destroy the possibility of the daisy's life. But these brawny and furious powers are ordered to bend themselves carefully to the needs of the most delicate structures; and every flower is so nice an index of the adjustment between the forces of the universe, that one might believe, looking at it exclusively, the globe and the solar system were built by the almighty as a factory to turn out the violets which embroider the spring.

from Music

Nature in her music seems to strive simply to set us the example of pure tone, smooth swell in volume, and delicate cadence and vanish. Listen to the elocution of the sea as it talks with the shore, and find how mellow, how utterly purged of all coarseness the serried thunder of its ground swell is, and how gentle the lisp of its last ripple that runs up a mile, perhaps, in length, like an army of little white mice nibbling the sand as they advance. . . . Hear the melancholy crescendo of a gust through a brotherhood of pines, and with what exquisite art of gradation it sighs away into calm! Hark, in the summer to the sweet dactyls of the Peabody-bird, the Canada sweet-whistler in the mountain valleys, and admire the smoothness of that high soprano, and how it slides and tapers into silence like the polished sting of the bee, in which the microscope can find no raggedness or flaw!

The most valuable lessons in the management of sound we must learn from Nature. And as to purity of tone, we must stand reverent, in the religious sense, before what she teaches us. For in this, as in the clearness of clouds and the transparency of air and the blaze of the sea-foam and the sparkle of moving rivers, she suggests to us the purity and holiness of God.

CHARLES LAMB

Lamb (1775-1834) was a popular English essayist of his time, known for his witty Essays of Elia. In the following excerpt, he takes a more satirical view of nature than that of his friend, the critic William Hazlitt.

from Popular Fallacies: That We Should Rise with the Lark

At what precise minute that little airy musician doffs his night gear, and prepares to tune up his unseasonable matins, we are not naturalists enough to determine. But for a mere human gentleman—that has no orchestra business to call him from his warm bed to such preposterous exercises—we take ten, or half after ten (eleven, of course, during the Christmas solstice), to be the very earliest hour at which he can begin to think of abandoning his pillow. To think of it, we say; for to do it in earnest requires another half hour's good consideration. Not but there are pretty sun-risings, as we are told, and such like gawds, abroad in the world, in summertime especially, some hours before what we have assigned; which a gentleman may see, as they say, only for getting up. But having been tempted once or twice, in earlier life, to assist at those ceremonies, we confess our curiosity abated. We are no longer ambitious of being the sun's courtiers, to attend at his morning levees. We hold the good hours of the dawn too sacred to waste them upon such observances; which have in them, besides, something Pagan and Persic. To say truth, we never anticipated our usual hour, or got up with the sun (as 'tis called), to go a journey, or upon a foolish whole day's pleasuring, but we suffered for it all the long hours after in listlessness and headaches; Nature herself sufficiently declaring her sense of our presumption in aspiring to regulate our frail waking course by the measures of that celestial and sleepless traveller. We deny not that there is something sprightly and vigorous at the outset especially, in these break-of-day excursions. It is flattering to get the start of a lazy world; to conquer death by proxy in his image. But the seeds of sleep and mortality are in us; and we pay usually, in strange qualms before night falls, the penalty of the unnatural inversion. Therefore, while the busy part of mankind are fast huddling on their clothes, are already up and about their occupations, content to have swallowed their sleep by wholesale; we choose to linger a-bed, and digest our dreams.

JANE LANGTON

Langton has been a member of the First Parish in Lincoln, Massachusetts, since 1950. Her mystery novels offer hints of her connection to Unitarian Universalism.

from The Transcendental Murder

The melting snow and the rains of March and April had swollen the river that flowed at the foot of the sprouting fields. But the weather of May and June, normally an occasion for irritation, abuse, misery, tears, pain, distress and withered hopes, had turned out so long and golden a succession of days that one almost forgot to take note any more or thank God or rejoice. It was like a king's grant, signed and sealed, or a special dispensation of

Providence. The greenish-white blossoming of Tom's trees was over now. It had been a spring when one walked carefully, afraid to tear or crush something incredible. But the most fragile time was past, and now there was strong ugly plantain in the grass.

Mary woke up on a Tuesday morning that was like the rest, clear and bright. Outside her bedroom window the fully-globed maple trees stood glittering like jeweler's work. In the elm tree a hoarse-throated bird had sprung a leak in his kettle and was dripping rusty splashes of song on the lawn. Mary got out of bed and pulled on her clothes, reflecting. It was the combination of things, perhaps, that had made it inevitable. Given a crop of young men with classical educations and given a succession of nurturing springtimes, how could New England *not* have produced a rash of transcendentalists? Or even so rare a flower as a Thoreau? Perhaps you shouldn't wonder at genius. Sometimes, maybe, it grew as naturally as weeds.

LEWIS H. LATIMER

Latimer (1848-1928) was one of the founding members of the Unitarian Church of Flushing, New York. The son of a runaway slave, he distinguished himself as inventor, patent expert, draftsperson, engineer, author, poet, and musician. His poetry was featured in the 1991 UUA meditation manual of African-American Unitarian Universalists, Been in the Storm So Long.

The Wanderer

A cold grey sky, a cold grey sea
And a cold grey mist is chilling me;
A light that burns on the harbor bar
With the dull dim glow of a distant star.
A sky without hope, a sea lacking cheer
And a beckoning light that comes not near;
The lapping of waves, the whisper of foam,
The gloom of night and a distant home.
What love can I feel for the restless sea
When all I love is leaving me!

The creak of a spar, the flap of a sail
Is far from a song since 'tis nearer a wail;
For the home and the friends that are leaving me
As I'm borne away o'er the cold grey sea.
A cold grey sky, a cold grey sea,
A distant land and a light to me
The only trace as I go my way
Of the joys and hopes of yesterday.
And I look on the sea, I turn to the sky
And they answer me life is mystery.

HENRY WADSWORTH LONGFELLOW

Longfellow (1807-1882) was raised "in the doctrine and spirit of the early Unitarianism," according to his brother Samuel, a Unitarian minister. Longfellow's works include the classics "Paul Revere's Ride" and "The Song of Hiawatha," which is among the works excerpted below.

from The Song of Hiawatha

Thus was Mudjekeewis chosen
Father of the Winds of Heaven.
For himself he kept the West-Wind,
Gave the others to his children;
Unto Wabun gave the East-Wind,
Gave the South to Shawondasee,
And the North-Wind, wild and cruel,
To the fierce Kabibonokka.
    Young and beautiful was Wabun;
He it was who brought the morning,
He it was whose silver arrows
Chased the dark o'er hill and valley;
He it was whose cheeks were painted
With the brightest streaks of crimson,
And whose voice awoke the village,
Called the deer, and called the hunter.
    Lonely in the sky was Wabun;

Though the birds sang gayly to him,
Though the wild-flowers of the meadow
Filled the air with odors for him;
Though the forests and the rivers
Sang and shouted at his coming,
Still his heart was sad within him,
For he was alone in heaven.

But one morning, gazing earthward,
While the village still was sleeping,
And the fog lay on the river,
Like a ghost, that goes at sunrise,
He beheld a maiden walking
All alone upon a meadow,
Gathering water-flags and rushes
By a river in the meadow.

Every morning, gazing earthward,
Still the first thing he beheld there
Was her blue eyes looking at him,
Two blue lakes among the rushes.
And he loved the lonely maiden,
Who thus waited for his coming;
For they both were solitary,
She on earth and he in heaven.

And he wooed her with caresses,
Wooed her with his smile of sunshine,
With his flattering words he wooed her,
With his sighing and his singing,
Gentlest whispers in the branches,
Softest music, sweetest odors,
Till he drew her to his bosom,
Folded in his robes of crimson,
Till into a star he changed her,
Trembling still upon his bosom;
And forever in the heavens
They are seen together walking,
Wabun and the Wabun-Annung,
Wabun and the Star of Morning.

The Harvest Moon

It is the Harvest Moon! On gilded vanes
   And roofs of villages, on woodland crests
   And their aerial neighborhoods of nests
   Deserted, on the curtained window-panes
Of rooms where children sleep, on country lanes
   And harvest-fields, its mystic splendor rests!
   Gone are the birds that were our summer guests;
   With the last sheaves return the laboring wains!
All things are symbols: the external shows
   Of Nature have their image in the mind,
   As flowers and fruits and falling of the leaves;
The song-birds leave us at the summer's close,
   Only the empty nests are left behind,
   And pipings of the quail among the sheaves.

Snow-flakes

Out of the bosom of the Air,
   Out of the cloud-folds of her garments shaken,
Over the woodlands brown and bare,
   Over the harvest-fields forsaken,
     Silent and soft and slow
     Descends the snow.

Even as our cloudy fancies take
   Suddenly shape in some divine expression,
Even as the troubled heart doth make
   In the white countenance confession,
     The troubled sky reveals
     The grief it feels.

This is the poem of the air,
   Slowly in silent syllables recorded;
This is the secret of despair,
   Long in its cloudy bosom hoarded,
     Now whispered and revealed
     To wood and field.

FRANCIS PARKMAN

Parkman (1823-1893) traced the backgrounds for his histories of North America on extended treks in the wilderness. He was the son of the Rev. Francis Parkman, a leading minister of orthodox Unitarianism for his time.

from France and England in North America

To the Indian, the material world is sentient and intelligent. Birds, beasts, and reptiles have ears for human prayers, and are endowed with an influence on human destiny. A mysterious and inexplicable power resides in inanimate things. They, too, can listen to the voice of man, and influence his life for evil or for good. Lakes, rivers, and waterfalls are sometimes the dwelling-place of spirits; but more frequently they are themselves living beings, to be propitiated by prayers and offerings. The lake has a soul; and so has the river, and the cataract. Each can hear the words of men, and each can be pleased or offended. In the silence of a forest, the gloom of a deep ravine, resides a living mystery, indefinite, but redoubtable. Through all the works of Nature or of man, nothing exists, however seemingly trivial, that may not be endowed with a secret power for blessing or for bane.

Men and animals are closely akin. Each species of animal has its great archetype, its progenitor or king, who is supposed to exist somewhere, prodigious in size, though in shape and nature like his subjects. A belief prevails, vague, but perfectly apparent, that men themselves owe their first parentage to beasts, birds, or reptiles—as bears, wolves, tortoises, or cranes; and the names of the totemic clans, borrowed in nearly every case from animals, are the reflection of this idea.

An Indian hunter was always anxious to propitiate the animals he sought to kill. He has often been known to address a wounded bear in a long harangue of apology. The bones of the beaver were treated with especial tenderness, and carefully kept from the dogs, lest the spirit of the dead beaver, or his surviving brethren, should take offence.

BEATRIX POTTER

Potter (1866-1943) was the author and illustrator of the classic children's book The Tale of Peter Rabbit. *Potter's parents and grandparents were Unitarians, and in a spirit somewhat ahead of her time, she was free to attend the services of any church of her choosing and still state, "I shall always call myself a Unitarian."*

Letter to June Steel, May 8, 1933

Castle Cottage, Sawrey, near Ambleside
My dear June,

Thank you for your nice little letter —I am glad to hear you are getting on well at school. I will write to you while I remember a pleasant walk I took this afternoon in Mr Todd's [sic] big wood. But first I must tell you I heard a noise just now like somebody talking in the kitchen—there was Mr Drake Puddleduck and 6 Mrs Ducks *sitting* on the *mat* before the *kitchen fire*!! Our servant had gone out and left the back door open and it was raining very hard. But that is no excuse for ducks, they like rain. Had it been hens, or turkeys, I should not have been surprised. I said "Whatever are you doing here Mr Puddleduck?" And out they waddled in a hurry, Mrs Possy duck always last; she is quite blind of one eye She runs against apple trees etc, but she seems as fat as any, so I suppose she can find worms & corn to eat.

The woods are lovely now, wild cherry trees covered with blossom as white as snow, and violets and primroses and blue bells amongst the nut bushes. The deer have been making a noise at nights, they make a curious gruff barking noise like a dog that is very hoarse. I wanted to see them. It is a time of year when the stags have no horns. It is very strange their horns fall off in spring, and grow again.

First I saw lots of rabbits, big old rabbits, and tiny baby rabbits of all sizes. One was peeping out from the root of a big fir tree. I saw nothing of Tommy Brock or Mr Todd. I was looking out for Mr Todd because something carried off one of my young lambs into the wood. We were afraid others might be taken so I hung up an old jacket for a scarecrow— at least I did not hang it up, I folded it and put it down as if someone had taken their coat off while at work, and I moved it every few days to a fresh place, & Mr Todd kept away afterwards. I saw footmarks of deer. I saw Mr Todd's old house, long deserted; the walls made of sticks & bits of wood have gone; only the chimny [sic] stack is standing. A wood pigeon has a nest in a holly tree near the door way. I went on and I saw the stump and the fallen tree where Mr Todd sat and read the newspaper. I was getting tired and very warm and thought I would turn back, only I could hear a cock pheasant calling cuck! cuck! Cuck!! very excited and cross, so I knew there was something stirring. I saw two light coloured patches that moved beyond the nut bushes—light brown ends of deer. I wonder why they have a light patch at the tail end. They were reaching up, eating the young leaves on the ash and oak saplings. I stood quite still and watched them for a time then I climbed up a little hill in the wood and got a view sideways, looking down. The biggest deer were in front, five very big animals, taller than donkys [sic]. They are rather like donkies (how do you spell donkys at school?) only they are red brown and they have awfully thin legs. One of the young bucks had knobs about an inch long on his head that was the horns growing. He looked dirty, in fact I saw him splashing about in a bog, they often roll in the mud to get away from flies and midges.

I watched them for some time keeping behind them. When the stags have horns it is not safe to go near them as they sometimes run at people like a bull. They seem to think the woods belong to them. They wander about for miles and miles. I only saw 10, but sometimes there is a drove of 40. They can do a lot of mischief if they come out onto the turnips and potato crops. It was a pretty sight to see the herd of deer moving away slowly. They never took any notice of me.

I hope you are very well. It is sad times in the big world but we must learn our lessons and hope for better days to come. There are nice showers of rain here, plenty of grass for the lambs.

With much love to you and your Mother

yrs aff
Beatrix Potter

ELIZABETH ROGERS

Rogers is a British Unitarian and a contributor to Echoes: A Second Anthology of Prayers, Meditations, and Poems by Contemporary Unitarians, *published by the Unitarian Worship Sub-Committee of London.*

Through the earth I am aware

I am a part of the earth.
I am a part of the solid, unshakeable,
Immutable rock
Of the mountain;
A part of the stark, rainwashed slabs of slate,
A part of the walls of wet and weathering gritstone,
A part of the crumbling granite of shining boulders.
I am part of what makes
The green rounded hill
With its splashes of laughing yellow gorse.

Through the earth I am aware
of what I am:
All that is firmly fixed and endures forever,
All that is shifting imperceptibly,
Being gently folded and unfolded,
All that holds the possibility
Of shattering violence of eruption;
All that is contained in
Is, and Was, and Shall Be.

For such awareness, coming from the earth,
I give my thanks today
For the earth, and my part in it.

JANE RANNEY RZEPKA

Rzepka is a Unitarian Universalist minister. She is the author of the 1989 UUA meditation manual, A Small Heaven.

Frogs and Firm Foundations

When I remember growing up, I picture being outdoors. In Ohio for three days one week, our children, trudging through the deep crusty snow, got the tour. "This is where Mommy:

made pottery out of real mud/clay and baked it in the sun;

caught fifteen frogs in one day, and then wondered why;

felt the best, most trusted, swinging grapevine collapse over a ledge on an otherwise perfectly normal day;

followed a brook through the woods in search of the Erie Canal and—maybe—Japan;

discovered the strangest thing ever: echoes;

camped alone in the woods for as many days as she could without coming in, and once got hopelessly lost and lonely;

chewed on sassafras leaves and Allegheny birch twigs and thought everybody did—and don't they still taste good;

fell through the ice and was so damn cold;

found wild flowers that took her breath away, but kept it secret, feeling guilty that she didn't let the *Cleveland Plain Dealer* know;

swam in the river in the pitch dark with girlfriends, each with hair in gigantic rollers;

and played tough Saturday basketball with friends in a barn and nothing was more important."

The kids just looked at me, the way kids do. But to me the earth seemed more solid that day, and the foundations never seemed firmer.

MAY SARTON

Sarton has written a wide range of novels, poetry, journals, and memoirs.

First Snow

This is the first soft snow
That tiptoes up to your door
As you sit by the fire and sew,
That sifts through a crack in the floor
And covers your hair with hoar.

This is the stiffening wound
Burning the heart of a deer
Chased by a moon-white hound,
This is the hunt, and the queer
Sick beating of feet that fear.

This is the crisp despair
Lying close to the marrow,
Fallen out of the air
Like frost on the narrow
Bone of a shot sparrow.

This is the love that will seize
Savagely onto your mind
And do whatever he please,
This the despair, and a moon-blind
Hound you will never bind.

Old Trees

Old trees—
How exquisite the white blossom
On the gnarled branch!
Thickened trunk, erratic shape
Battered by winter winds,
Bent in the long cold.

Young ones may please
The aesthete,

But old trees—
The miracle of their flowering
Against such odds—
Bring healing.

Let us praise them.
And sing hosannahs
As the small buds grow red
Just before they open.

Summer Music

Summer is all a green air—
From the brilliant lawn, sopranos
Through murmuring hedges
Accompanied by some poplars;
In fields of wheat, surprises;
Through faraway pastures, flows
To the horizon's blues
In slow decrescendos.

Summer is all a green sound—
Rippling in the foreground
To that soft applause,
The foam of Queen Anne's lace.
Green, green in the ear
Is all we care to hear—
Until a field so suddenly flashes
The singing with so sharp
A yellow that it crashes
Loud cymbals in the ear.
Minor has turned to major
As summer, lulling and so mild,
Goes golden-buttercup-wild.

WILLIAM F. SCHULZ

A Unitaran Universalist minister, Schulz is the fifth President of the Unitarian Universalist Association.

from Unitarian Universalism in a New Key

Hundreds of years ago Saint Lawrence asked, "Whom should I adore: the Creator or the Creation?" Most Western religions have answered back, "Adore the Creator!" and supplied an image (Zeus, Jehovah, Christ) to be adored. But our answer is far different. Whom should we adore? The Creation, surely, for whatever there be of the Creator will be made manifest in Her handiwork.

"God," said Mies van der Rohe, "dwells in the details." The Divine for us—whatever it in essence be—is not confined to a transcendent realm, its ramparts guarded by the scholarly elite. On the contrary, the Holy is made manifest to every one of us—not just those who can recite the catechism—in the transactions of the Everyday. It lies curled, in other words, in the very bosom of our experience.

This is a fundamental departure from religion's preoccupation with abstraction. It is not a distant, mysterious God to whom we make appeal or even the cold vagaries of Progress, Evolution, Creativity, or History. The gods and goddesses—or, if you prefer, the most precious and profound—are accessible to us in the taste of honey and the touch of stone.

And this in turn is why we love the earth, honor the human body, and bless the stars. Religion is not just a matter of Things Unseen. For us the Holy is not hidden but shows its face in the blush of the world's exuberance.

HENRY DAVID THOREAU

Thoreau (1817-1862) was raised a member of the First Parish of Concord, Massachusetts, but signed off after leaving college in 1837. He remained a key figure in the Transcendentalist movement, publishing Walden, or Life in the Woods *in 1854.*

from Walden

Near the end of March, 1845, I borrowed an axe and went down to the woods by Walden Pond, nearest to where I intended to build my house, and began to cut down some tall arrowy white pines, still in their youth, for timber. It is difficult to begin without borrowing, but perhaps it is the most generous course thus to permit your fellow-men to have an interest in your enterprise. The owner of the axe, as he released his hold on it, said that it was the apple of his eye; but I returned it sharper than I received it. It was a pleasant hillside where I worked, covered with pine woods, through which I looked out on the pond, and a small open field in the woods where pines and hickories were springing up. The ice in the pond was not yet dissolved, though there were some open spaces, and it was all dark colored and saturated with water. There were some slight flurries of snow during the days that I worked there; but for the most part when I came out on to the railroad, on my way home, its yellow sand heap stretched away gleaming in the hazy atmosphere, and the rails shone in the spring sun, and I heard the lark and the pewee and other birds already to commence another year with us. They were pleasant spring days, in which the winter of man's discontent was thawing as well as the earth, and the life that had lain torpid began to stretch itself. One day, when my axe had come off and I had cut a green hickory for a wedge, driving it with a stone, and had placed the whole to soak in a pond hole in order to swell the wood, I saw a striped snake run into the water, and he lay on the bottom, apparently without inconvenience, as long as I staid there, or more than a quarter of an hour; perhaps because he had not yet fairly come out of the torpid state. It appeared to me that for a like reason men remain in their present low and primitive condition; but if they should feel the influence of the spring of springs arousing them, they would of necessity rise to a higher and more ethereal life. I had previously seen the snakes in frosty mornings in my path with portions of their bodies still numb and inflexible, waiting for the sun to thaw them. On the 1st of April it rained and melted the ice, and in the early part of the day, which was very foggy, I heard a stray goose groping about over the pond and cackling as if lost, or like the spirit of the fog.

So I went on for some days cutting and hewing timber, and also studs and rafters, all with my narrow axe, not having many communicable or scholar-like thoughts, singing to myself—

Men say they know many things;
But lo! they have taken wings—
The arts and sciences,
And a thousand appliances;
The wind that blows
Is all that any body knows.

* * *

I went to the woods because I wished to live deliberately, to front only the essential facts of life, and see if I could not learn what it had to teach, and not, when I came to die, discover that I had not lived. I did not wish to live what was not life, living is so dear; nor did I wish to practise resignation, unless it was quite necessary. I wanted to live deep and suck out all the marrow of life, to live so sturdily and Spartan-like as to put to rout all that was not life, to cut a broad swath and shave close, to drive life into a corner, and reduce it to its lowest terms, and, if it proved to be mean, why then to get the whole and genuine meanness of it, and publish meanness to the world; or if it were sublime, to know it by experience, and be able to give a true account of it in my next excursion. For most men, it appears to me, are in a strange uncertainty about it, whether it is of the devil or of God, and have *somewhat hastily* concluded that it is the chief end of man here to "glorify God and enjoy him forever."

from A Week on the Concord and Merrimack Rivers

You shall see men you never heard of before, whose names you don't know, going away down through the meadows with long ducking-guns, with water-tight boots wading through the fowl-meadow grass, on bleak, wintry, distant shores with guns at half-cock, and they shall see teal, blue-winged, green-winged, shelldrakes, whistlers, black ducks, ospreys, and many other wild and noble sights before night, such as they who sit in parlors never dream of. You shall see rude and sturdy, experienced and wise men, keeping their castles, or teaming up their summer's wood, or chopping alone in the woods, men fuller of talk and rare adventure in the sun and wind and rain, than a chestnut is of meat; who were out not only in '75 and 1812, but have been out every day of their lives; greater men than Homer, or Chaucer, or Shakespeare, only they never got time to say so; they never took to the way of writing. Look at their fields, and imagine what they might write, if ever they should put pen to paper. Or what have they not written on the face of the earth already, clearing, and burning, and scratching, and harrowing, and ploughing, and subsoiling, in and in, and out and out, and over and over, again and again, erasing what they had already written for want of parchment.

JACOB TRAPP

Trapp has a long and distinguished career as poet, minister, and thinker. His books include Dawn to Dusk, Light of a Thousand Suns, *and* To Hallow This Life, *an anthology of the work of theologian Martin Buber. He is minister emeritus of the Unitarian Church in Summit, New Jersey.*

from Lilac, Thrush, and Western Star

The twig of lilac suggests many things—the new life blossoming forth from the old, birth, rebirth, resurrection, the unsullied fresh loveliness of childhood; the elusive, indescribable uniqueness of the person. In Salt Lake City they showed me a letter about the person for whom we were about to hold a memorial service. It told of her good work for this organization and that organization. We were all sort of grasping at crumbs or straws of expression for something that could not be said but which was yet very vivid and close and alive to all of us—that subtle uniqueness and loveliness of the person, as real and like itself and indescribable as the lilacs which at that very moment were in bloom near the kitchen door.

The thrush, in Isaiah's language, represents beauty for ashes, the oil of joy for mourning, the garment of praise for the spirit of heaviness. The poet praises the twin sisters Birth and Death for the gifts of life and love they carry between them. The thrush means music, and the curious and fathomless fact that without suffering there would be no song.

The evening star in the West, shall we say, represents greatness, the kind of human greatness that moves and exalts us as we are attracted to it. It also means that we are not to leave the sky out of our landscape; that the simplest things of earth speak to us of something from beyond. The western star, shall we say, represents this awareness of transcendence, also the living transcendence expressed in beauty, in music, and in greatness— a star that may disappear over the horizon, but that returns as the earth turns, and is always there.

JONES VERY

Very (1813-1880) was a radical Unitarian minister for his time. He often experienced intense periods of religious exaltation. William Cullen Bryant and Ralph Waldo Emerson are among those who praised his work.

The Homeless Wind

Where has thou been roaming,
    Thou houseless, homeless wind?
Thy voice is sad and moaning,
    Thou hast none of thy kind.

WIND.

I've been in lone places,
    Upon the wild sea-shore,
Where billow billow chases,
    And listened to their roar.

I saw the sailor tossing
    Upon the stormy sea;
He sighed, while ocean crossing,
    In sympathy with me.

I've heard the roar of battle,
    And soldier's dying wail;

Men fell, like herds of cattle,
    Beneath War's leaden hail.

I've been on the high hilltop,
    And on the lonely plain:
Where'er I roamed, I could not stop
    Contented to remain.

For still that wail pursued me,
    More sad and deep than mine;
No sounds upon the land or sea
    Its sadness can define.

But now around man's dwelling,
    From places lone and drear,
My story I've been telling,
    But found I none to hear.

For no one there had feeling
    For the houseless, homeless wind,
To receive its sad revealing
    In sympathy of mind.

KURT VONNEGUT

Vonnegut is a novelist and social critic. Of his religious views, he has said, "The Army decided my religion was "P," for Protestant. There is no room on dogtags for footnotes and a bibliography."

from Galapagos

As luck would have it, there was going to be a documentary about the lives of blue-footed boobies on the islands shown on educational television that evening, so King enclosed notes saying that they might want to watch it. These birds would later become crucial to the survival of the little human colony on Santa Rosalia. If those birds hadn't been so stupid, so incapable of learning that human beings were dangerous, the first settlers would almost certainly have starved to death.

The high point of that program, like the high point of Mary Hepburn's lectures on the islands at Ilium High School, was film footage of the courtship dance of the blue-footed boobies. The dance went like this:

There were these two fairly large sea birds standing around on the lava. They were about the size of flightless cormorants, and had the same long, snaky necks and fish-spear beaks. But they had not given up on aviation, and so had big, strong wings. Their legs and webbed feet were bright, rubbery blue. They caught fish by crashing down on them from the sky. Fish! Fish! Fish!

They looked alike, although one was a male and the other was a female. They seemed to be on separate errands, and not interested in each other in the least— although there wasn't much business for either one of them to do on the lava, since they didn't eat bugs or seeds. They weren't looking for nesting materials, since it was much too early in the game for that.

The male stopped doing what he was so busy doing, which was nothing. He caught sight of the female. He looked away from her, and then back again, standing still and making no sound. They both had voices, but at no point in the dance would either make a sound.

She looked this way and that, and then her gaze met his accidentally. They were then five meters apart or more.

When Mary showed the film of the dance at the high school, she used to say at this point, as though she were speaking for the female: "What on Earth could this strange person want with me? Really! How bizarre!"

The male raised one bright blue foot. He spread it in air like a paper fan.

Mary Hepburn, again in the persona of the female, used to say, "What is that supposed to be? A Wonder of the World? Does he think that's the only blue foot in the islands?"

The male put that foot down and raised the other one, bringing himself one pace closer to the female. Then he showed her the first one again, and then the second one again, looking her straight in the eye.

Mary would say for her, "I'm getting out of here." But the female didn't get out of there. She seemed glued to the lava as the male showed her one foot and then the other one, coming closer all the time.

And then the female raised one of her blue feet, and Mary used to say, "You think you've got such beautiful feet? Take a look at this, if you want

43

to see a beautiful foot. Yes, and I've got another one, too."

The female put down one foot and raised the other one, bringing herself one pace closer to the male.

Mary used to shut up then. There would be no more anthropomorphic jokes. It was up to the birds now to carry the show. Advancing toward each other in the same grave and stately manner, neither bird speeding up or slowing down, they were at last breast to breast and toe to toe.

At Ilium High School, the students did not expect to see the birds copulate. The film was so famous, since Mary had shown it in the auditorium in early May, as an educational celebration of springtime, for years and years, that everybody knew that they would not get to see the birds copulate.

What those birds did on camera, though, was supremely erotic all the same. Already breast to breast and toe to toe, they made their sinuous necks as erect as flagpoles. They tilted their heads back as far as they would go. They pressed their long throats and the undersides of their jaws together. They formed a tower, the two of them—a single structure, pointed on top and resting on four blue feet.

Thus was a marriage solemnized.

ROBERT R. WALSH

Walsh is a Unitarian Universalist minister. He is the author of the 1992 UUA meditation manual, Noisy Stones.

Interruption

On US-30, west of Gettysburg, I saw a dead deer beside the road. I sped on past. I had hundreds of miles to go that day. Then I felt called back. I made a U-turn on the four-lane highway and returned to the deer.

It was early on a Sunday morning. There was little traffic.

I approached and crouched beside the body. His eyes were open. I imagined for a moment that he was still alive, but there was no movement, no breath. I had been drawn to the deer by reverence and awe, but these gave way initially to curiosity and amateur forensic analysis.

One of his hind legs was broken, with the bone sticking out. There was a pool of dark blood under his head. There was a trail of blood about thirty feet long from the near lane of the highway. There were bony stubs where his antlers had been. I guessed he had been hit by a car, had died of a head injury, and had been dragged by someone to the shoulder of the road. I guessed the antlers had been taken for souvenirs.

I touched his side, his face, his broken leg. I sat with him for a minute or two, then decided to move him off the shoulder and into the underbrush. I pulled him by his forelegs, dragging him over and down a six-foot bank. I covered him with large leaves of weeds that grew there.

I said a prayer. I apologized for the system, my system, of people and machines and roads that had brought his meaningless death. I apologized for the indifference, which I have shared, that had brought his mutilation. I gave thanks for having found the courage to stop and to touch him.

I returned to my car and resumed my journey south.

LINDA WELTNER

Weltner is a free-lance writer and columnist for The Boston Globe. *She is the author of* No Place Like Home: Rooms and Reflections from One Family's Life, *a collection of essays.*

A Valentine to the Whole Universe

I think the universe wants to attract us. By the myriad life forms it contains, by the fossil treasures it has hidden within rock for us to find, by its refusal to fully conform to our scientific formulas, it has already become the object of our intense fascination. But I'm beginning to think that it's after more than our curiosity, that it desires our devotion, even our adoration. After all, if a member of the opposite sex showered us with such gifts, wouldn't we suspect that he was trying to win us over with fields of flowers, captivate us with seashells, and seduce us with snowflakes?

Not all valentines come in the shape of hearts.

Cosmologist Brian Swimme says that one of the underlying principles of the universe is communion, the way in which all aspects of creation are in profound relationship to one another. It is this communion aspect of existence that allows us to digest plants, to decipher the language of people halfway around the world, to have love affairs with our pets. It's why we thrill to the sight of snowtopped mountains when we might just as easily be indifferent. We come with an inborn response to nature that requires only the right stimulus to leap into being. That's the reason that all it takes to convince humankind of the value of whales is to give enough people a glimpse of one.

I used to think I appreciated the natural world. I've always been grateful to the earth, that long-suffering old soul, and when I read about massive oil spills in the ocean, I felt horror and pity as well. I recycle out of a mixture of duty and enlightened self-interest. I know there's too much garbage to dispose of by throwing it all away, and clearly, when the planet's health is in danger, so is mine. For all those reasons, I counted myself a friend of the earth.

But something in me changed the other night. The sight of the stars elicited in me memories of a whole series of ecstatic events: the time my husband and I got soaked to the skin hiking and entering into a world of mist and shadow at dusk, felt ourselves a part of the wilderness at Yosemite; the time my friend Lynn and I decided to fling ourselves into the huge waves created by a hurricane offshore, and our egos melted away in the crashing and tumbling of the surf; the time I took a nap in a field in Vermont and, half awake, heard the buzzing of the flies and the murmur of the wind in the grass the way a deer might.

These moments of merger have been some of the most fulfilling experiences of my life. In hindsight, I see them as early episodes in an ongoing romance of which I was unaware. Until the North Star looked down from the sky and pierced my consciousness with its gaze, I hadn't allowed these times of passionate communion with nature to awaken me to my true relationship with the universe. It's hard to put my feeling into words, but it would be harder to write this if I weren't so sure my feelings were reciprocated.

I'm in love.

WILLIAM CARLOS WILLIAMS

Williams (1883-1963) was a doctor, as well as a Pulitzer Prize-winning poet. His parents helped found a Unitarian society in Rutherford, New Jersey, and he described his early religious education in his autobiography: "It appealed to me that Christ was divine by the spirit that was in him and not by miraculous birth. This seemed democratic and to the point. I believed it."

The Widow's Lament in Springtime

Sorrow is my own yard
where the new grass
flames as it has flamed
often before but not
with the cold fire
that closes round me this year.
Thirtyfive years
I lived with my husband.
The plumtree is white today
with masses of flowers.
Masses of flowers
load the cherry branches
and color some bushes
yellow and some red
but the grief in my heart
is stronger than they
for though they were my joy
formerly, today I notice them
and turn away forgetting.
Today my son told me
that in the meadows,
at the edge of the heavy woods
in the distance, he saw
trees of white flowers.
I feel that I would like
to go there
and fall into those flowers
and sink into the marsh near them.

Flowers by the Sea

When over the flowery, sharp pasture's
edge, unseen, the salt ocean

lifts its form—chicory and daisies
tied, released, seem hardly flowers alone

but color and the movement—or the shape
perhaps—of restlessness, whereas

the sea is circled and sways
peacefully upon its plantlike stem

N.[EWELL] C.[ONVERS] WYETH

Wyeth (1882-1945) was an active member of the First Unitarian Society in Wilmington, Delaware. Although famous for his paintings and illustrations, Wyeth reveals a profound sympathy with the natural world, especially in his early letters. He saw the earth as only a painter could.

Letter to Stimson (Babe) Wyeth, August 16, 1908

Chadds Ford, Pennsylvania
Dear Babe,

Talk about thunderstorms!!! The one we have just had, the past hour and a half, makes the one that blew in the day you were here look like Aunt Hat doing fancy work on the front lawn.

About four o'clock I went over back of Sheatz's barn to make a study of some haystacks—it looked a trifle threatening in the south and it *did* manage to pee a bit, but it didn't bother me with my work. All of a sudden I noticed a peculiar livid yellow striking on Taylor's hill (I was facing east); I turned, and just over the brink of a big bare hill behind me I saw a long black edge of a cloud—black, as I never saw it before. I continued with my sketching for a few moments, but was forced to stop on account of the yellow that gradually slid down Taylor's hill and transformed the entire background of my picture.

That *yellow* puzzled me! I could see nothing but black behind me, so packing up my paint box, I struck out for the top of the hill.

What I saw looked truly unnatural: a clean, straight, vivid strip of burnished-gold sky—positively *metallic*, which reflected a gorgeous glow of gold-bronze over the western slopes. The hills appeared as though one were looking through stained glass at them—so intense was the light.

It looked foreboding! So I struck out for home.

The black cloud grew to tremendous proportions, its upper edges tattered and wisplike. The yellow streak remained the same—a blinding garish light. The distant hills started to deepen into wonderful inky purples and the foreground looked green— a *poison* green, and the buildings in the village stood out hard and edgy like toy blocks, painted yellow, red, white and blue. Little people started to run back and forth, pigeons darted like white specter-spots against the black sky, cattle and horses looked impatient and walked nervously about. Suddenly, the distant trees changed from their deep sodden green into silvery greens and whites, the whole landscape seemed to awaken with a shudder. One could hear a soft rush, as of distant water; gradually it grew louder and louder and without warning the wind was upon us! Dust flew! Fallen leaves sailed high in the air like live things, trees swayed and bended, the grass flattened to the ground, and above all, great mountains of purple and black clouds hurtled through the sky. The distant band of yellow became darkened like tarnished brass. Peal upon peal of low, rumbling thunder trembled the air and in the distant sky the fork lightning streaked to the earth in fantastic tracings.

What followed I can hardly describe! A pandemonium of wind, rain, livid flashes of lightning and thunder that cracked in quick succession. The air flared with treacherous bolts that seethed and crashed like hellish serpents and the house trembled and shook in the tumult. One's very head became dizzy and the walls of the house seemed to melt in the livid flashes!

The rain poured down in sheets and it was dark as night.

This continued for three-quarters of an hour without abating. Gradually the western horizon lighted up dully and the good sunlight shown through the still-pouring rain, making it look like bronze, getting brighter and brighter until the sky scintillated with the golden drops of rain.

I don't know that I ever felt more grateful to the sun in my life! After such a terrifying storm! to go out onto the open field (and I had Henriette on my shoulder) to look down upon the shining valley with its river and broad quiet meadows, and the cows peacefully feeding, the fresh green grass sparkling with the wet, the fragrance of soaked earth in the air—how grateful I felt for it! Not that I feared my safety through the storm, but to witness such a mighty and terrible battle of nature, and then to see her come up serene and smiling!

Letter to Stimson (Babe) Wyeth, June 11, 1909

Chadds Ford, Pennsylvania

Dear Babe,

The main theme of this afternoon's visions lies in one very strange, and to you, intangible detail.

A fresh breeze blowing through the pine boughs, along the river somewhere—most likely through one of those big pines up at the oaks. The point of view seems to be from the ground. I lie on my back looking up at the heavy green foliage of needles slowly lifting and lowering against the bright but somewhat gray sky; I watch the changing shapes of light as it breaks through the moving branches; the beauty of the tree's construction losing itself in the deep shadowy dome of green fascinates me. The great mystery of earth and sky, the profundity of the infinite depths shining between those swaying branches impresses me and like soft exquisite music the lap-lap-lap-lap of the rippling river reaches my ears. My whole soul is atingle! My imagination is on fire! The universe towers in my mind a great overpowering mystery. The significance of the tiniest speck of bark on the pine tree assumes the proportions of the infinite sky; my brain almost bursts with the effort to really appreciate the meaning of *life*, of *existence!* I reach a pinnacle of thought and my mind collapses—I watch the swaying tree and I hear the lap-lap-lap of the water—I thank fate that I was brought into this life—I ardently promise, with all my soul, to do my best, to make my short life of use, to add an infintesimal might to the world!!

WHITNEY MOORE YOUNG, JR.

Young (1921-1971) was a social worker, educator, and activist, and a member of the Community Unitarian Church in White Plains, New York. Young was the Executive Director of the National Urban League from 1961 to 1971. The following parable is taken from his sociological work, To Be Equal.

from To Be Equal

A farmer, hunting in the woods one day, came across an eagle chick, recently hatched. He carried the eaglet back to his farm and put it in with the other barnyard fowl. Here it stayed for a year and grew alongside the chickens and geese. One day a passing naturalist saw the eagle among the other fowl and berated the farmer for raising the eagle with the chickens. The farmer, in all innocence, said, "He has been raised with the barnyard fowl. To all intents and purposes he is one and is happy so."

The naturalist offered to prove that this was not true and for several hours coaxed the eagle to fly. However, the eagle reacted as if it were a chicken, hopping to the ground and scratching for food. Finally the naturalist took the eagle to the top of a nearby mountain. Holding the bird high above his head and over the valley below, he spoke to it: "Eagle you are and eagle you will always be. You were born to soar in the skies, not to scratch in the dust. Lift your wings and fly!" At this the eagle trembled as if new life had come into him; the powerful wings beat, tentatively at first, then with strength, and off he flew, disappearing into the horizon, never to return. It *was* an eagle, though it had been raised as a chicken.

I have related this anecdote to audiences of young Negroes and I have concluded it with these words: "Though you have been humiliated and deprived, suggesting you are a nobody, you are *really* somebody. Though you have been segregated and discriminated against, which would imply that you are a second-class citizen, you are *really* a first-class human being. Stretch your minds, lift your sights, and fly."

ACKNOWLEDGMENTS

Many of the selections in this book were made possible by the kind permission of the following authors and/or publishers: Sara Moores Campbell, for "The Growing Season," Skinner House Books, 1990. Liveright Publishing Corporation, for "maggie and milly and molly and may" and "i thank you God for most this amazing," E.E. Cummings, *Complete Poems 1913-1962.* Excerpt from *All I Really Need to Know I Learned in Kindergarten* by Robert Fulghum. © 1986, 1988 by Robert Fulghum. Reprinted by permission of Villard Books, a division of Random House. Jane Langton, for excerpt from *The Transcendental Murder*, Harper and Row, 1964. The Toronto Public Library, the Osbourne Collection of Early Children's Books, for Beatrix Potter's letter to June Steel, May 8, 1933. W. W. Norton & Company, for "First Snow," "Summer Music," and "Old Trees" from *Sarton Selected: An Anthology of the Journals, Novels, and Poems of May Sarton*, by May Sarton, edited by Bradford Dudley Daziel, copyright W. W. Norton & Company, 1991. Kurt Vonnegut, for excerpt from *Galapagos*, Delacorte Press/Seymour Lawrence, 1985. Robert R. Walsh, for "Interruption," from *Noisy Stones*, Skinner House Books, 1992. William Carlos Williams: *The Collected Poems of William Carlos Williams, 1909-1939, vol. 1.* Copyright 1938 by New Directions Publishing Corporation. Reprinted by permission of New Directions Publishing Corporation. Excerpts from *The Wyeths*, by N. C. Wyeth, edited by Betsy James Wyeth. Copyright © 1971 by Betsy James Wyeth. Whitney Moore Young, *To Be Equal*, 1964, McGraw-Hill, Inc. Reproduced with permission of McGraw-Hill, Inc.

6onfig